Art of Swear

Swear Word Adult Coloring Book

By

B. Nozz

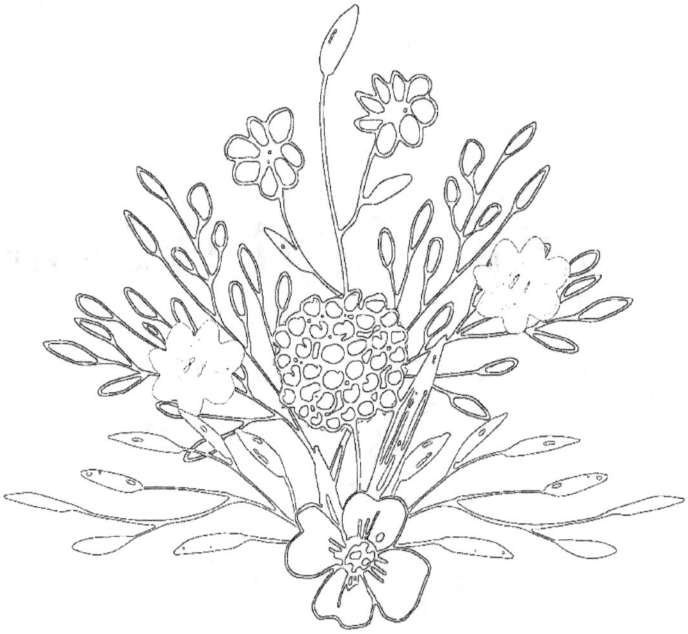

Happy Coloring!

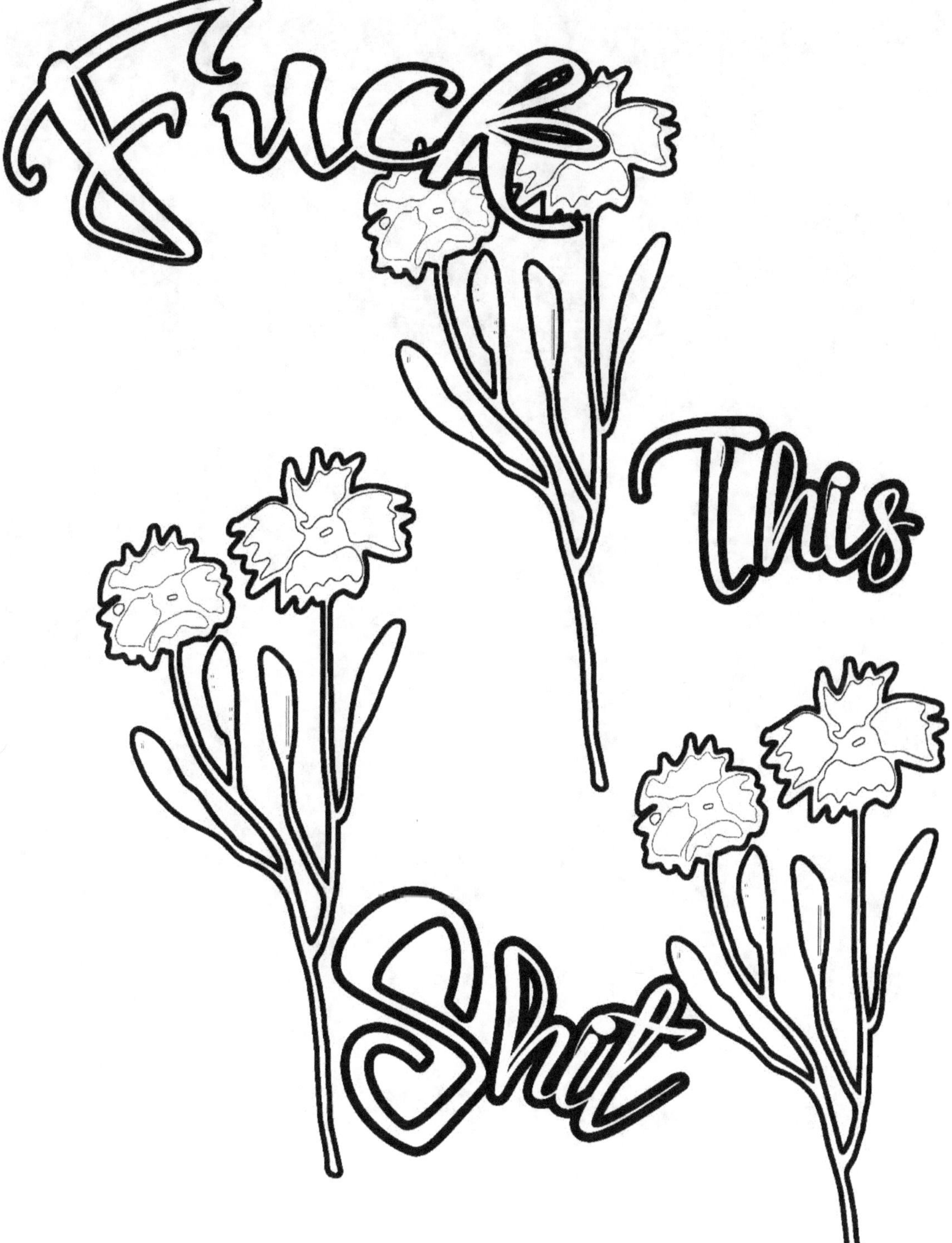
Fuck
This
Shit

Old Fart

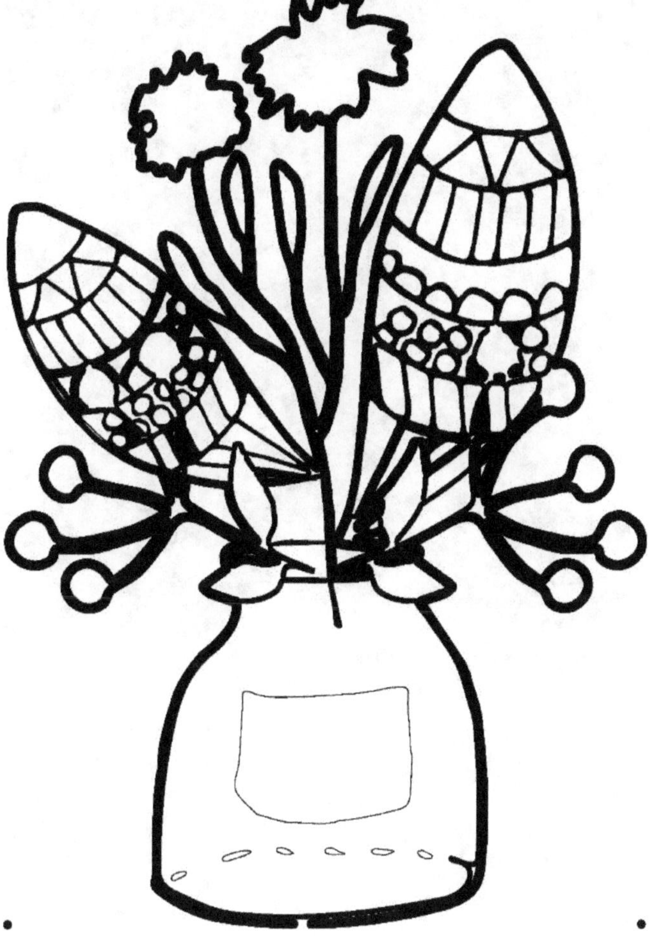

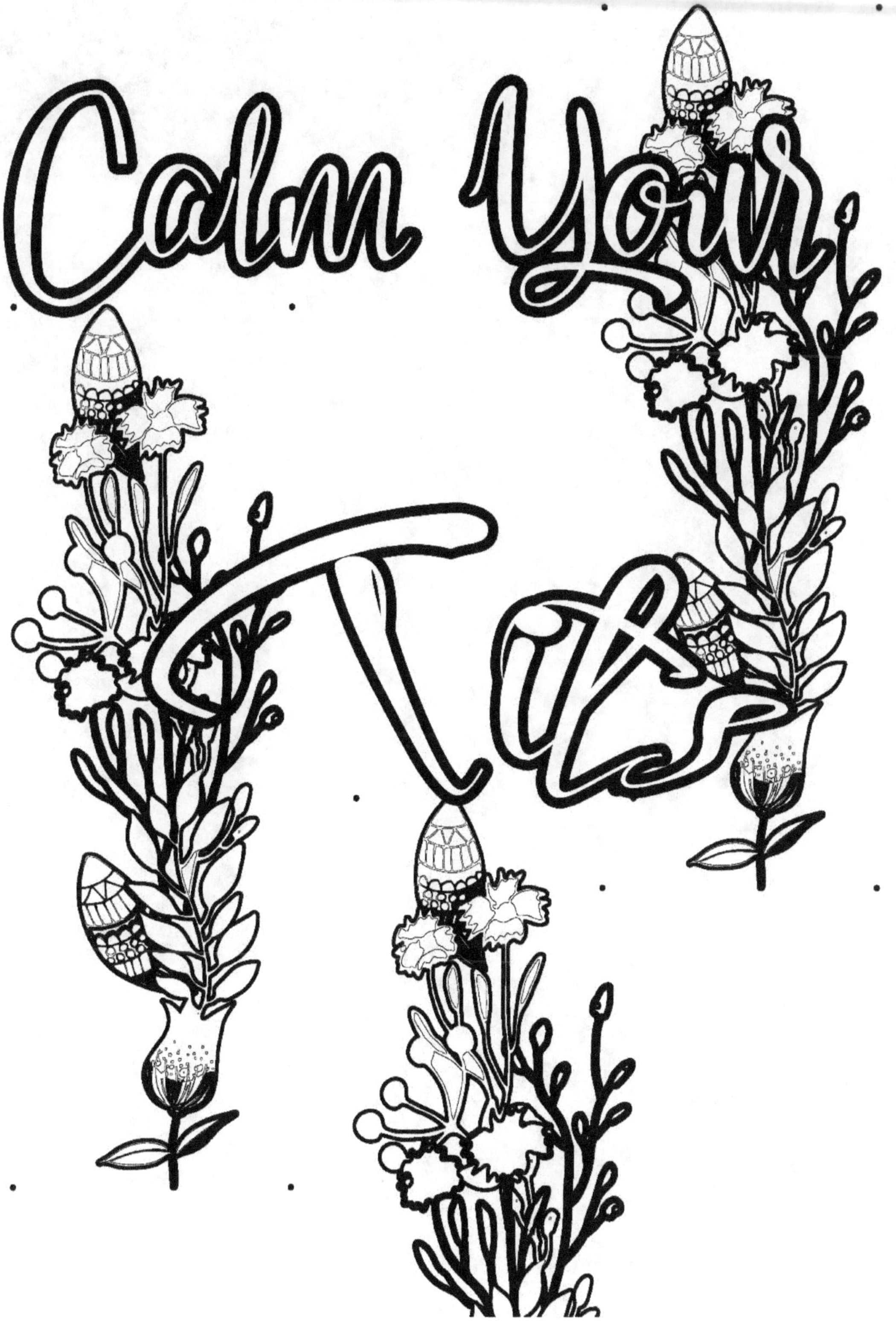
Calm Your
Tits

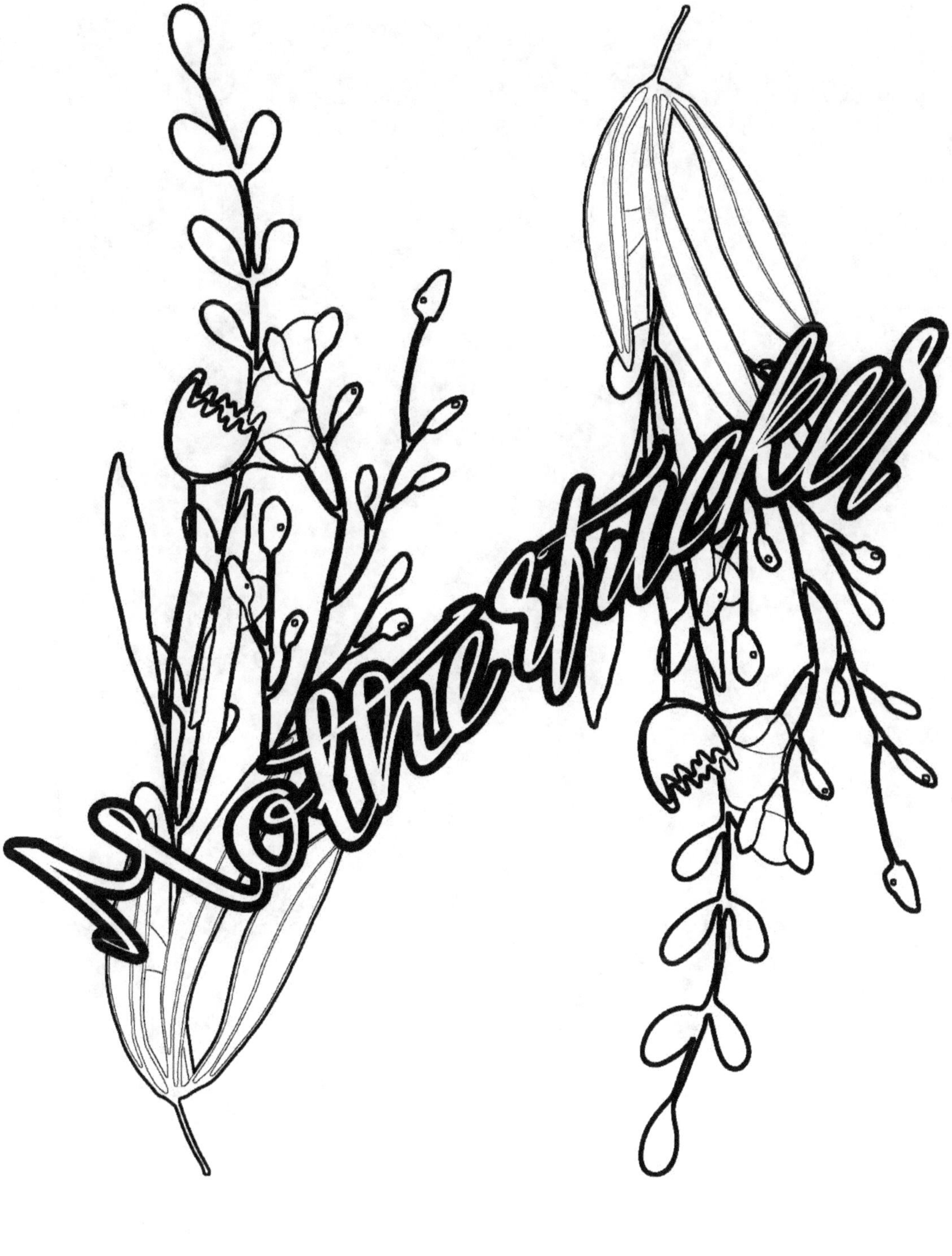
Motherfucker

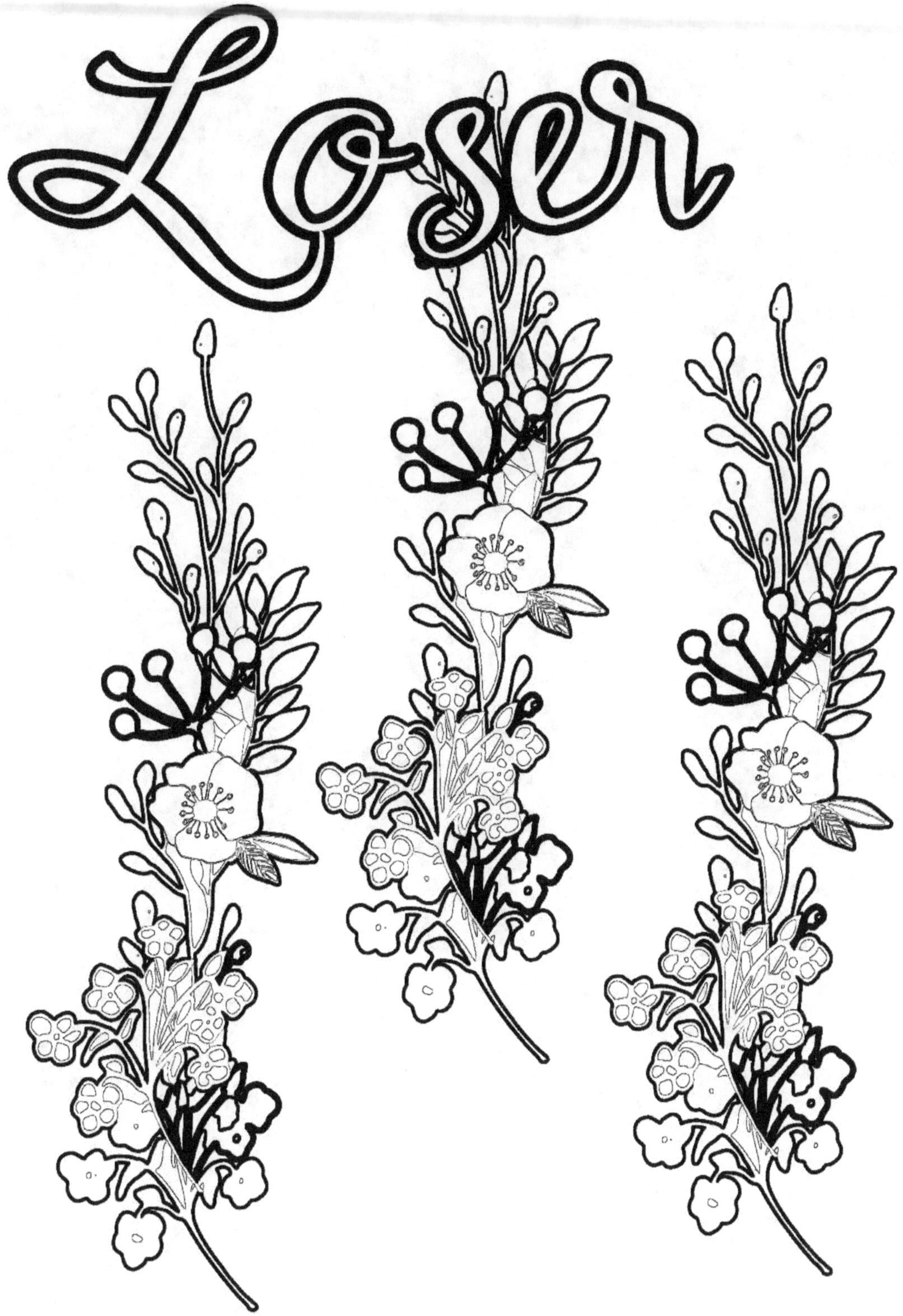
Loser

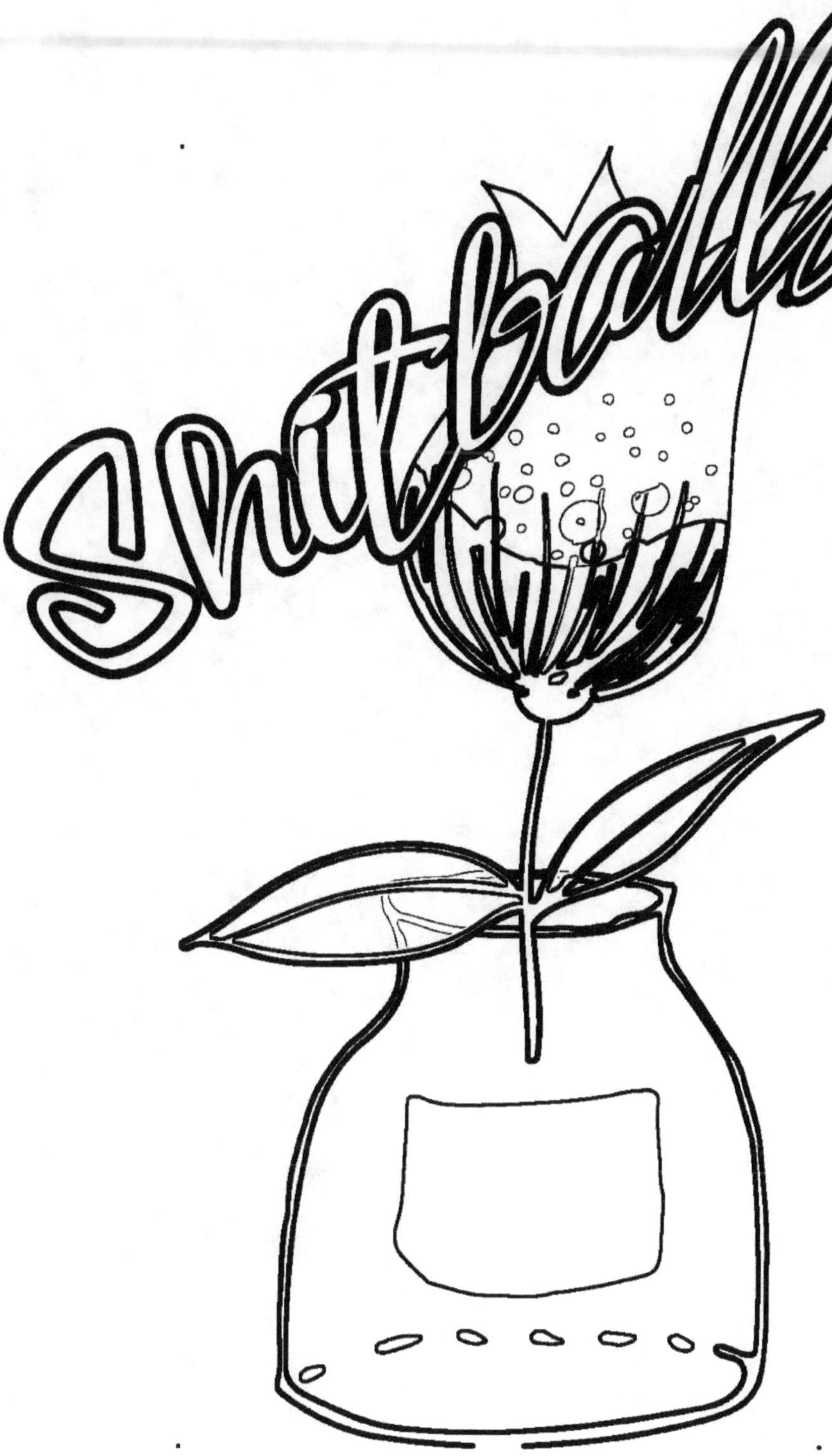
Shitballs

Shitfaced

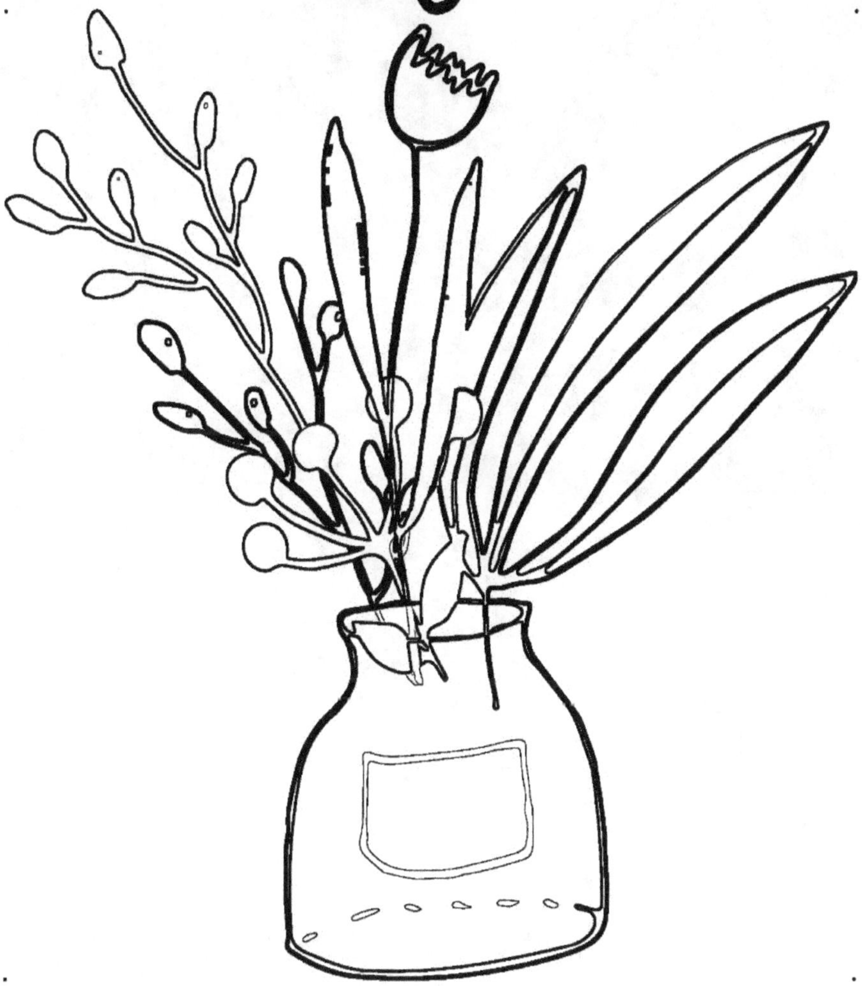

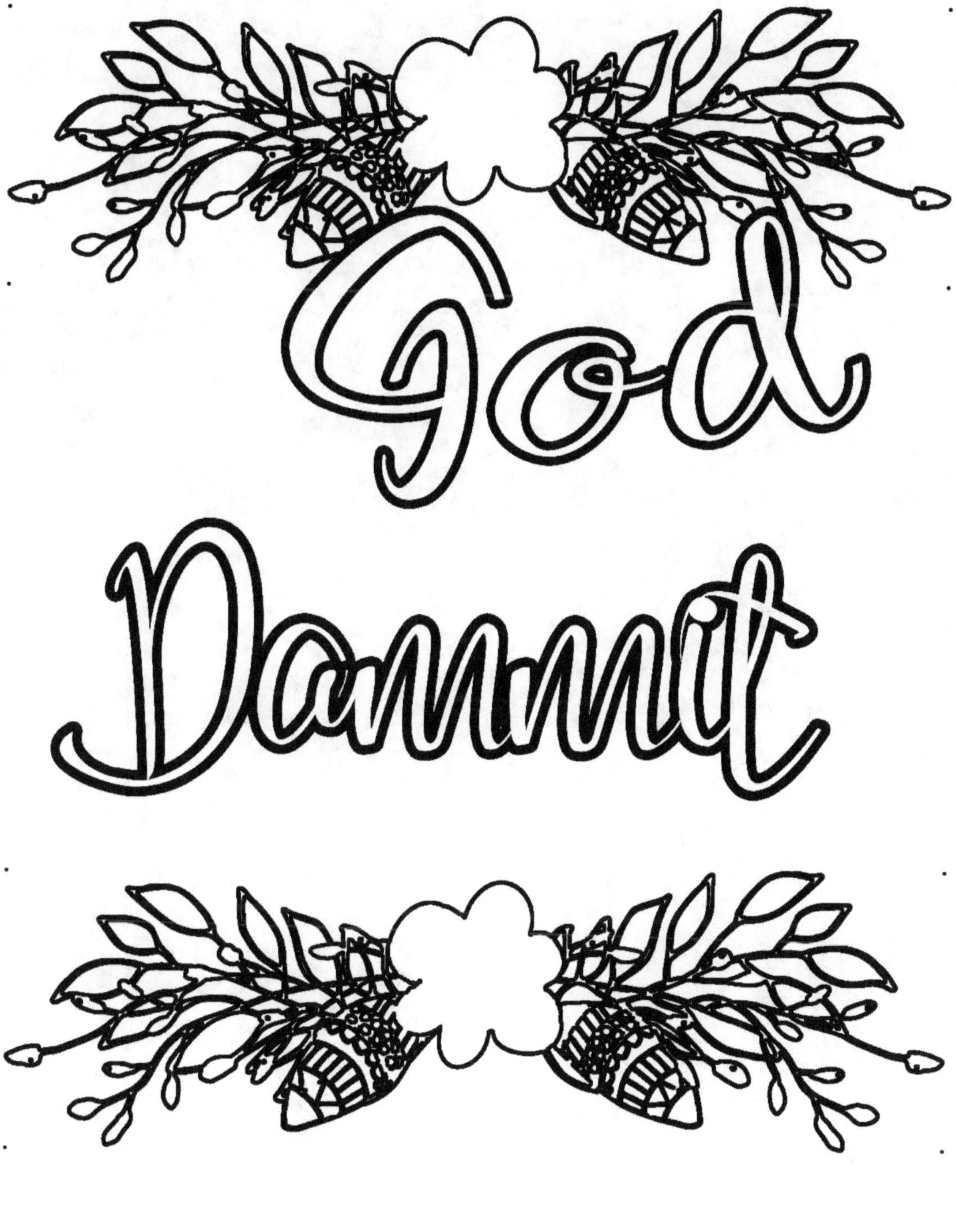
God
Dammit

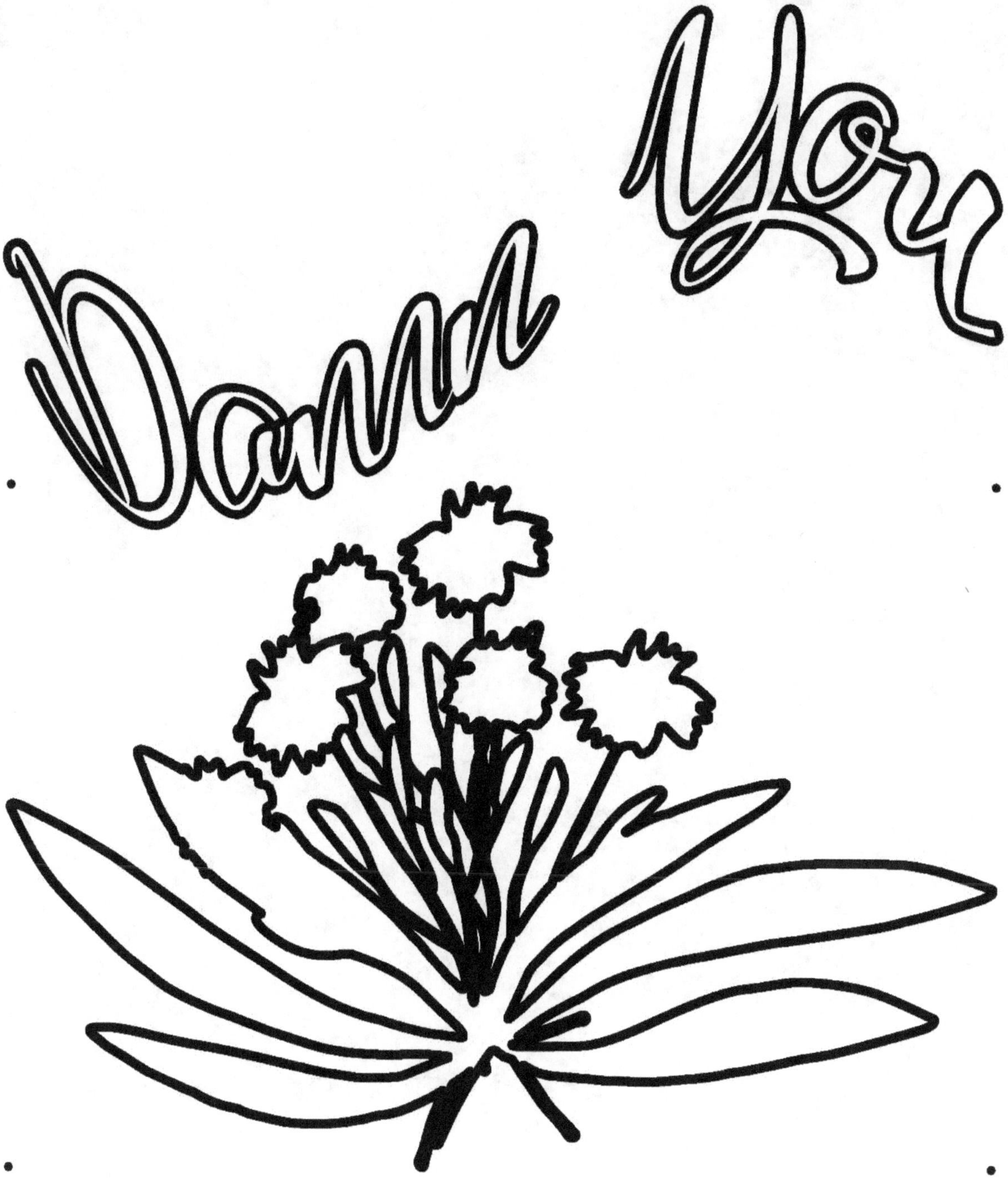
Damn You

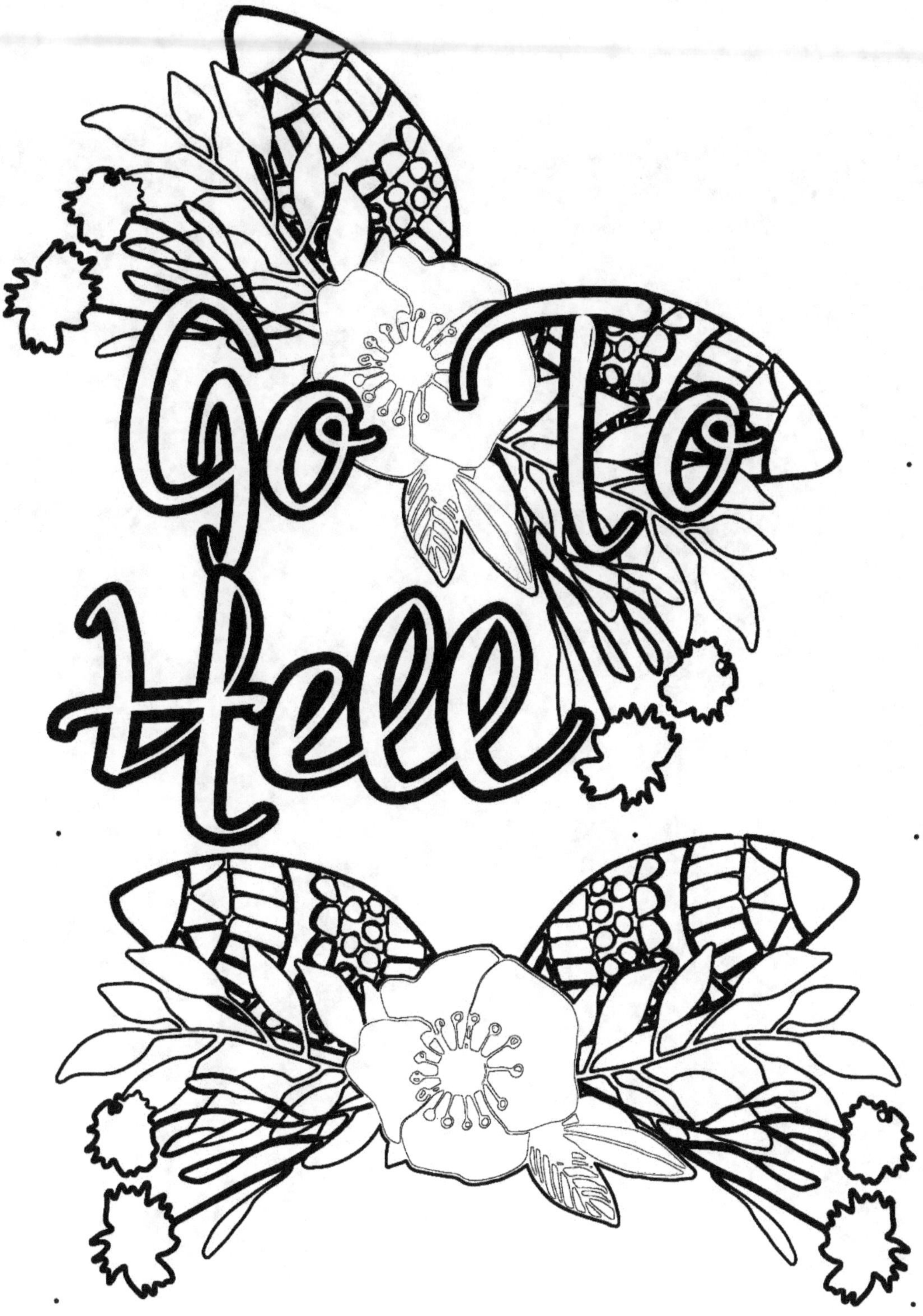
Go To
Hell

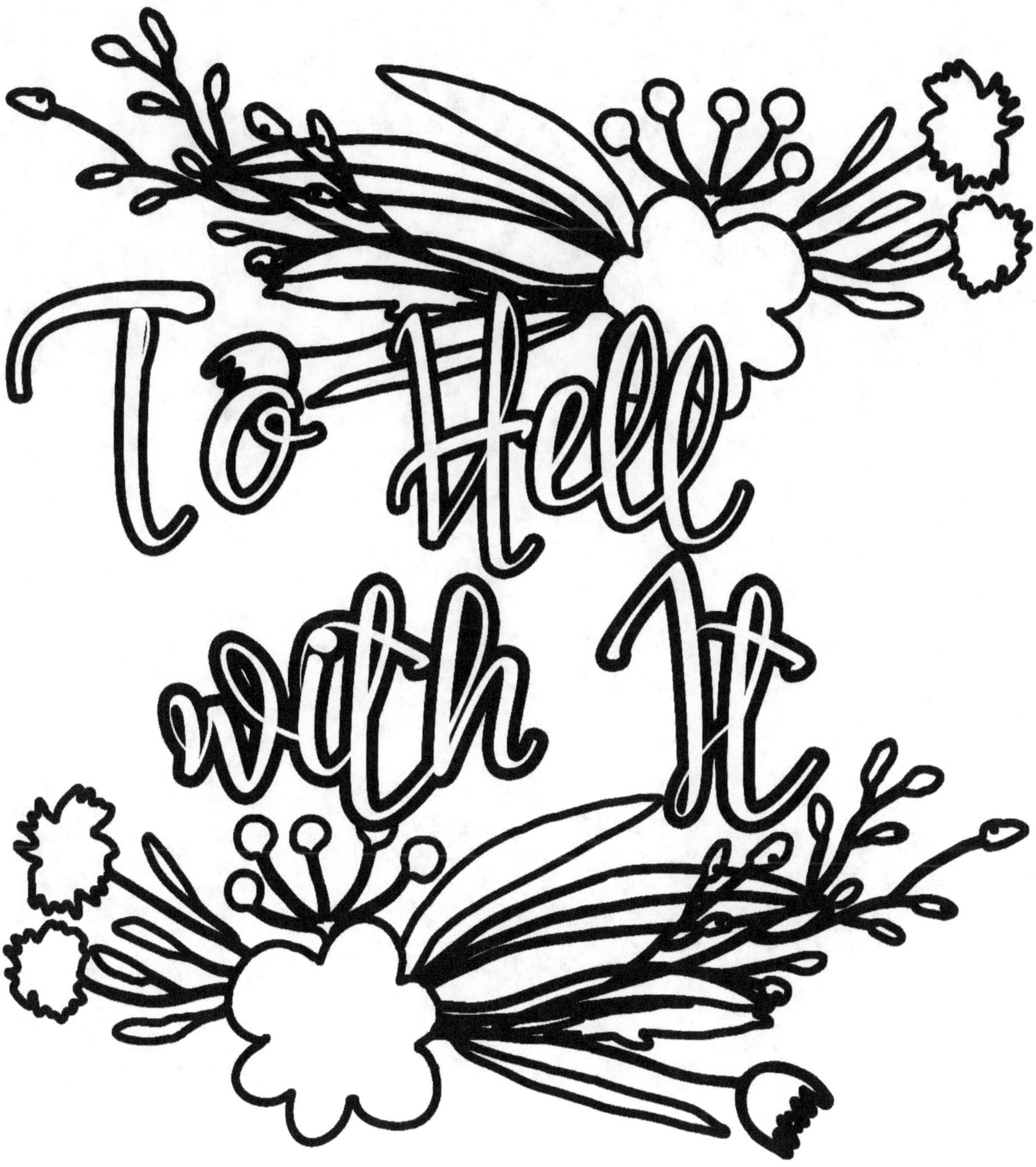
To Hell
with It

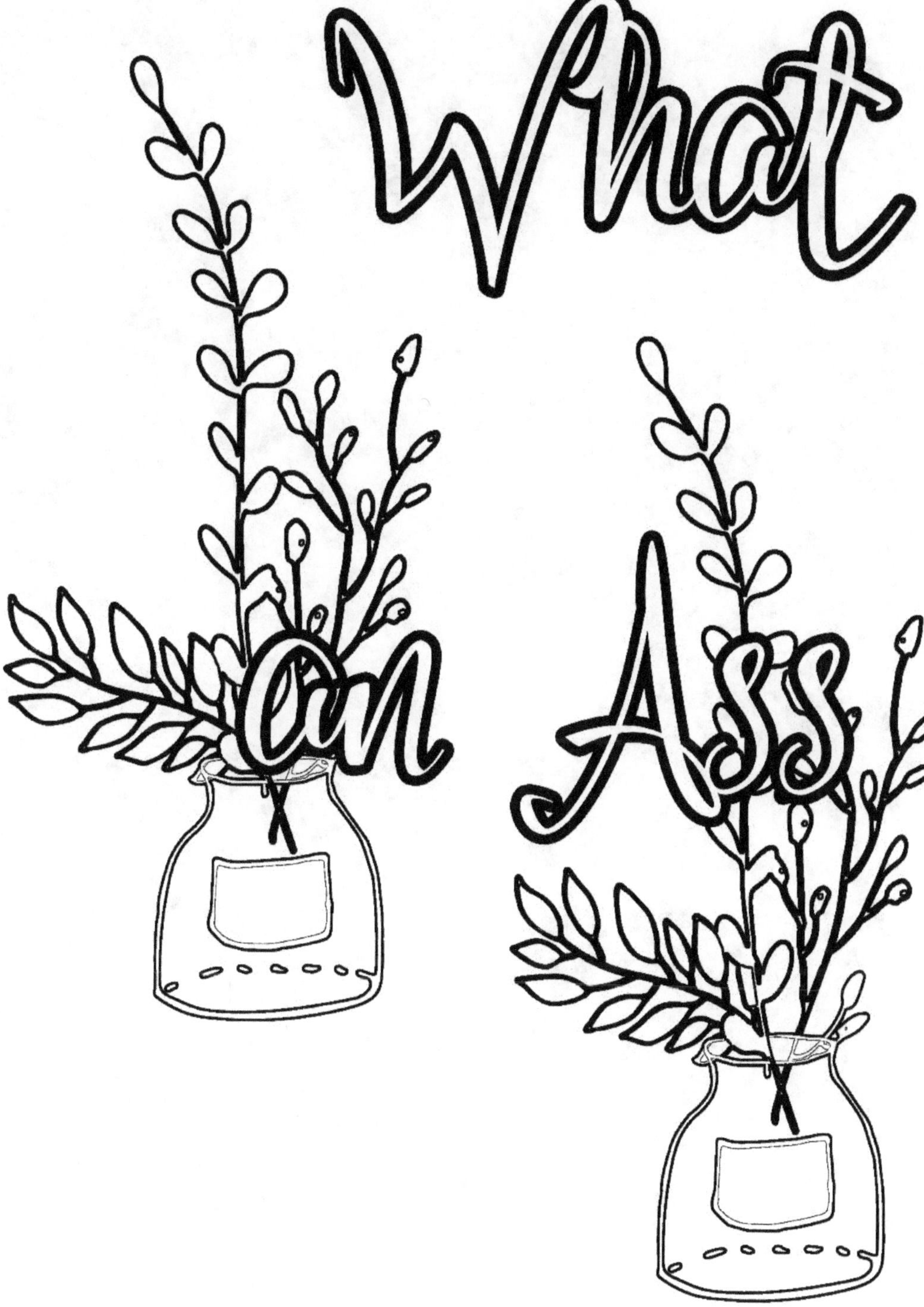
What
an Ass

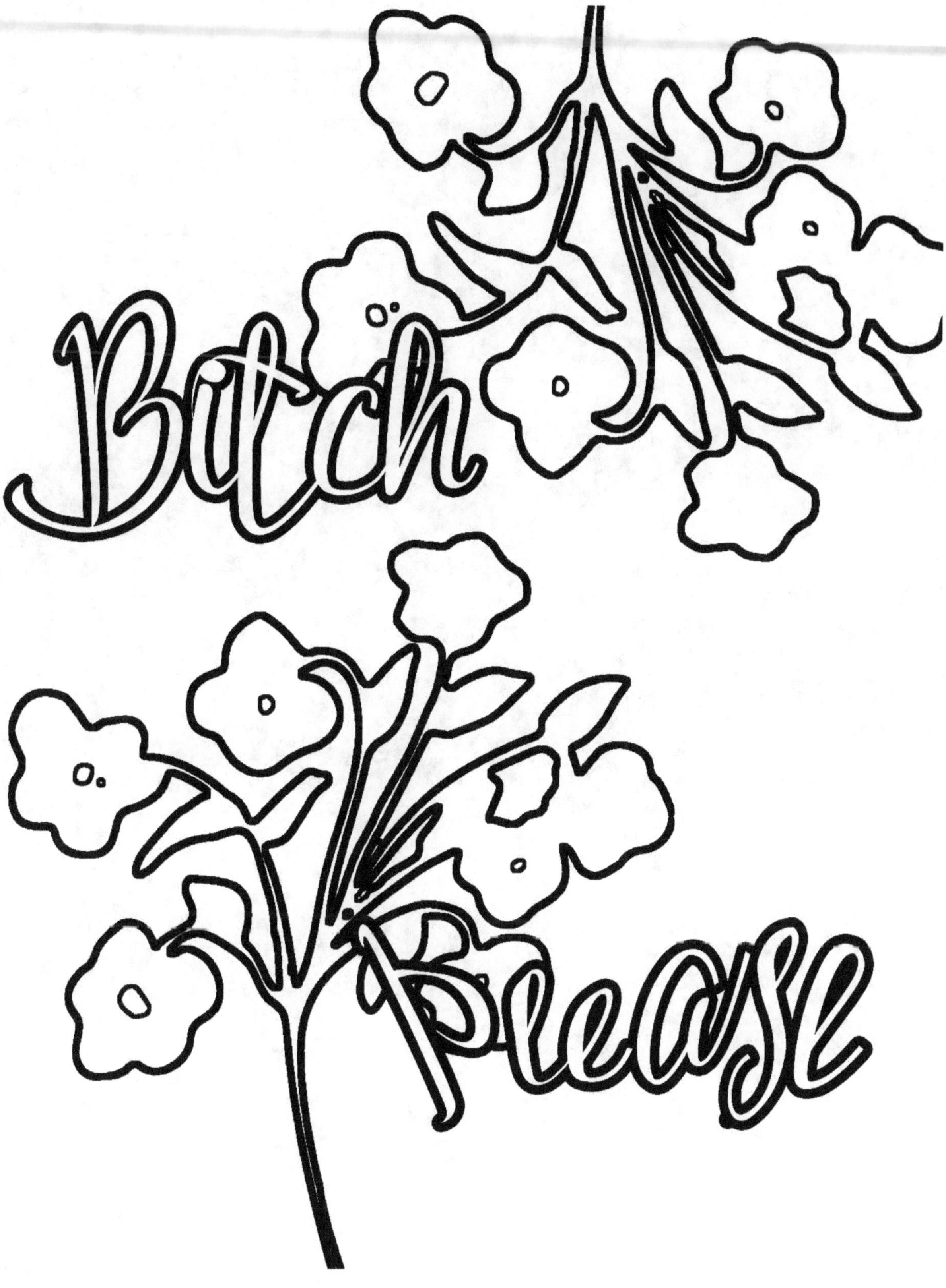
Bitch
Please

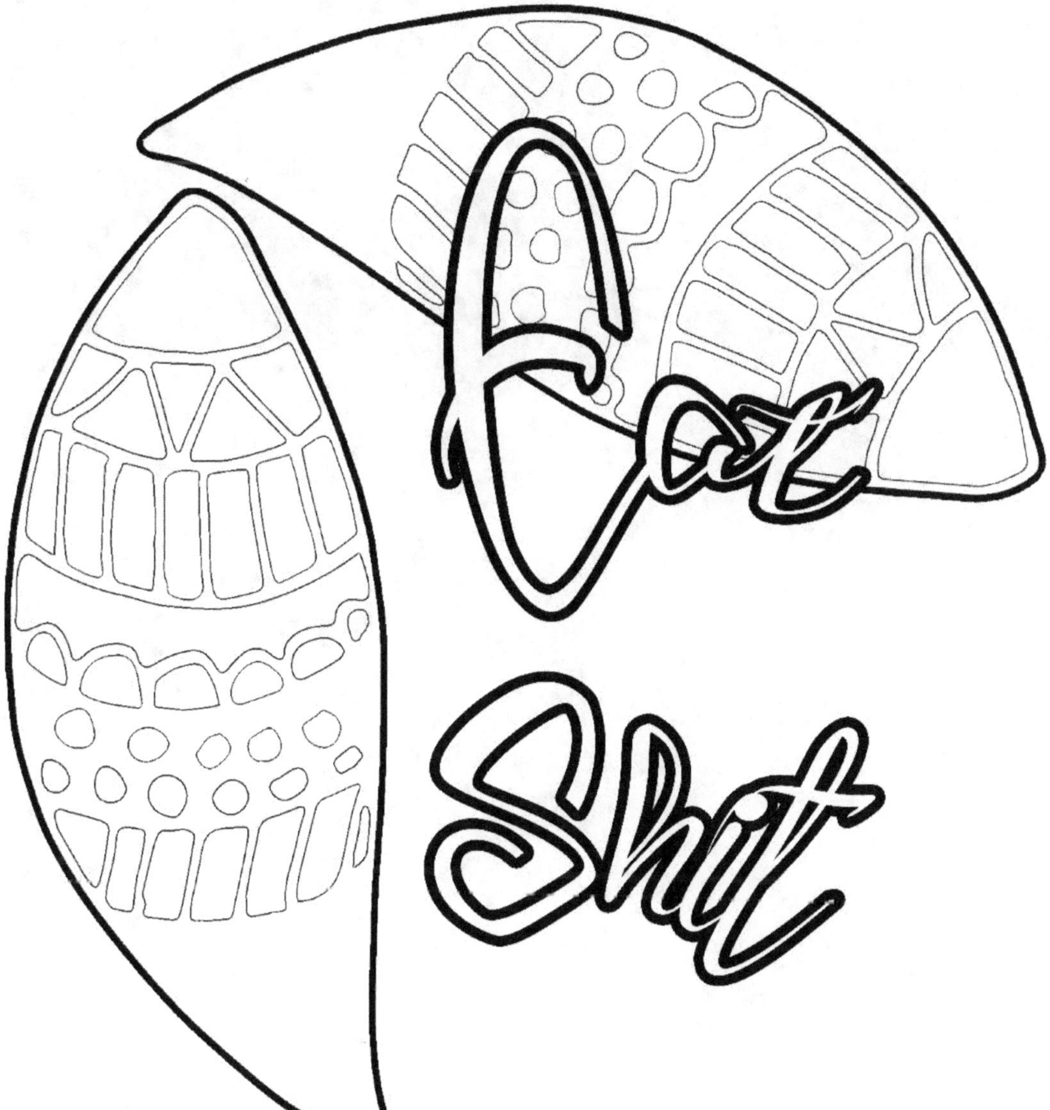
Eat
Shit

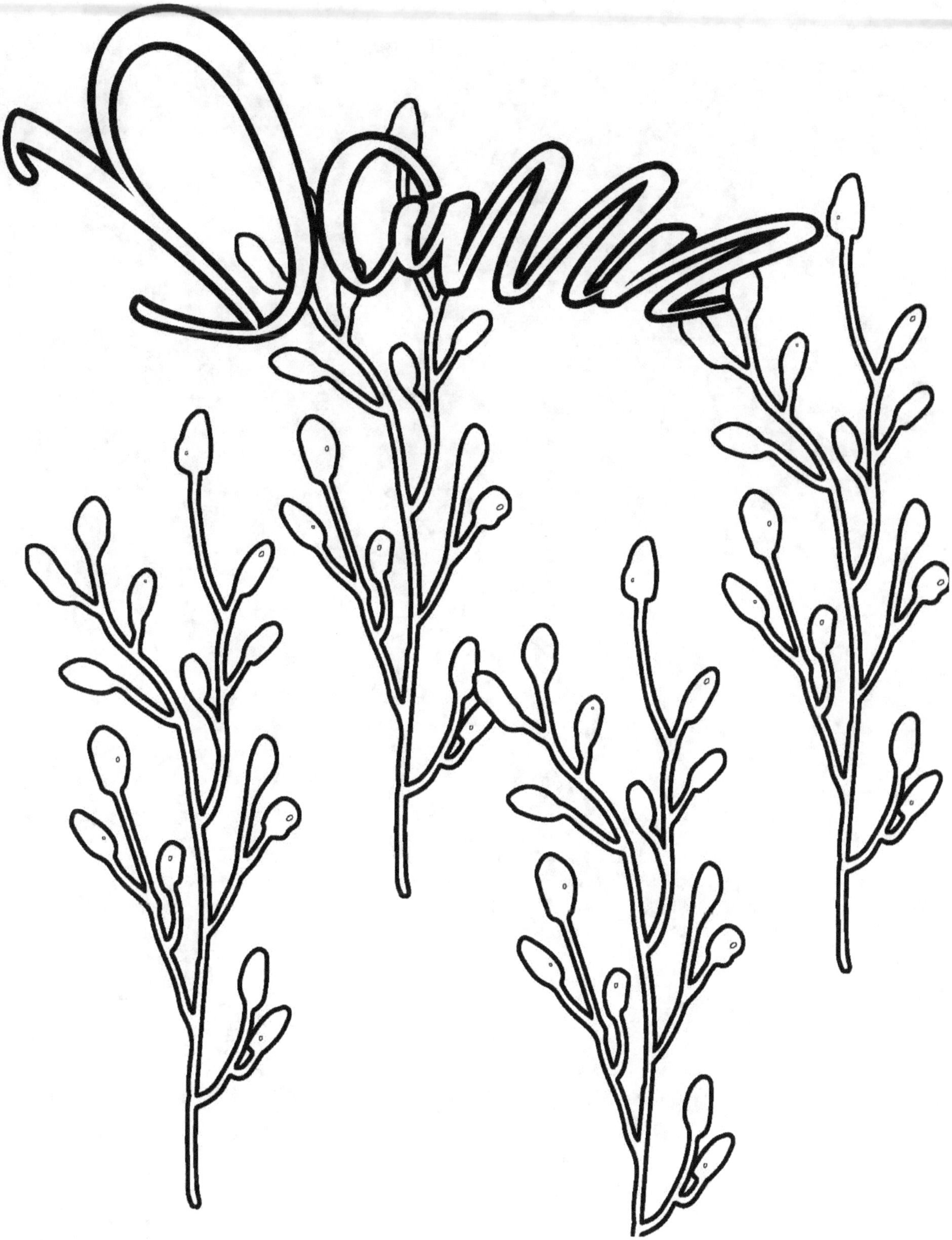
Damn

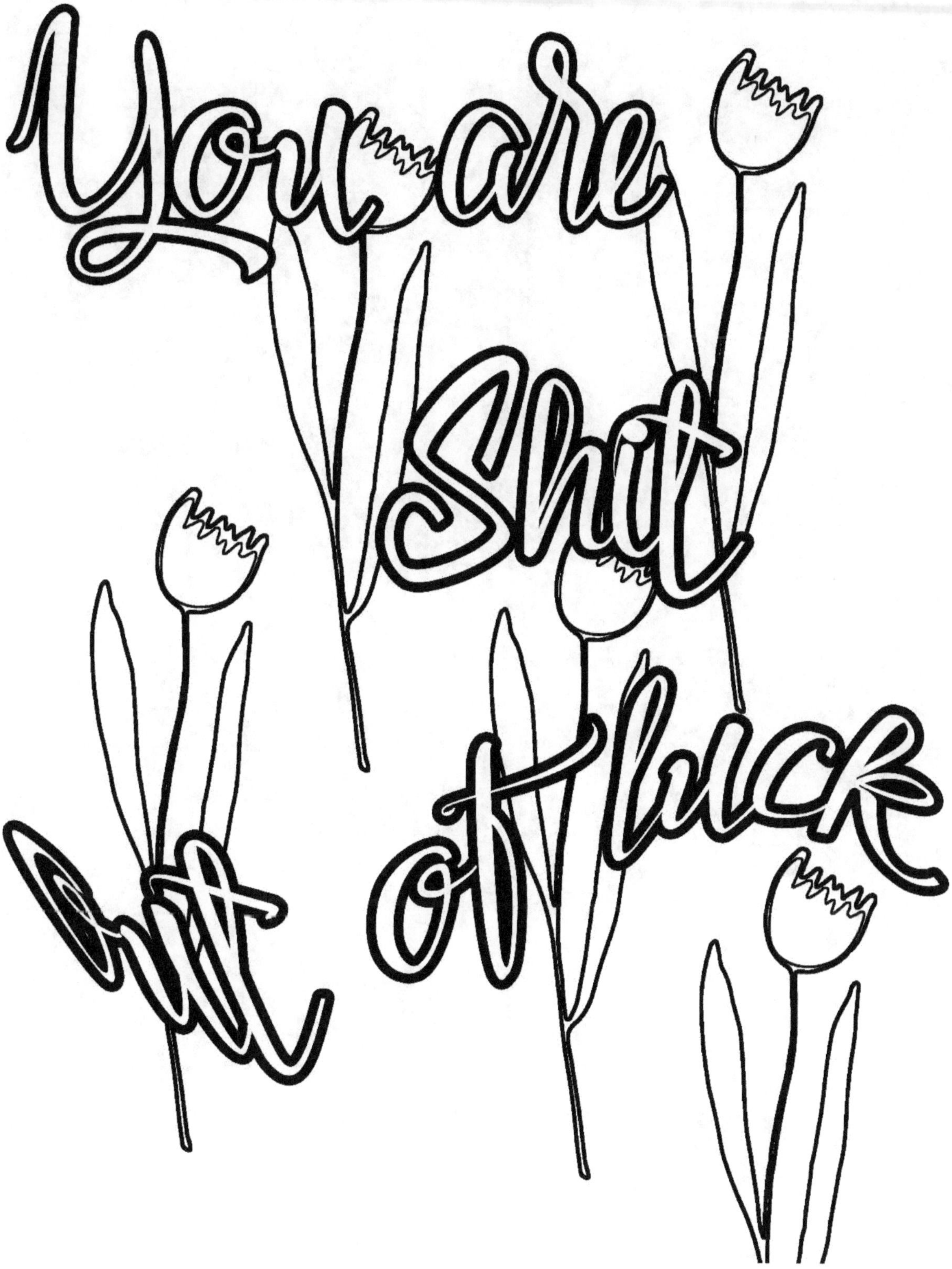
You are
Shit
out of luck

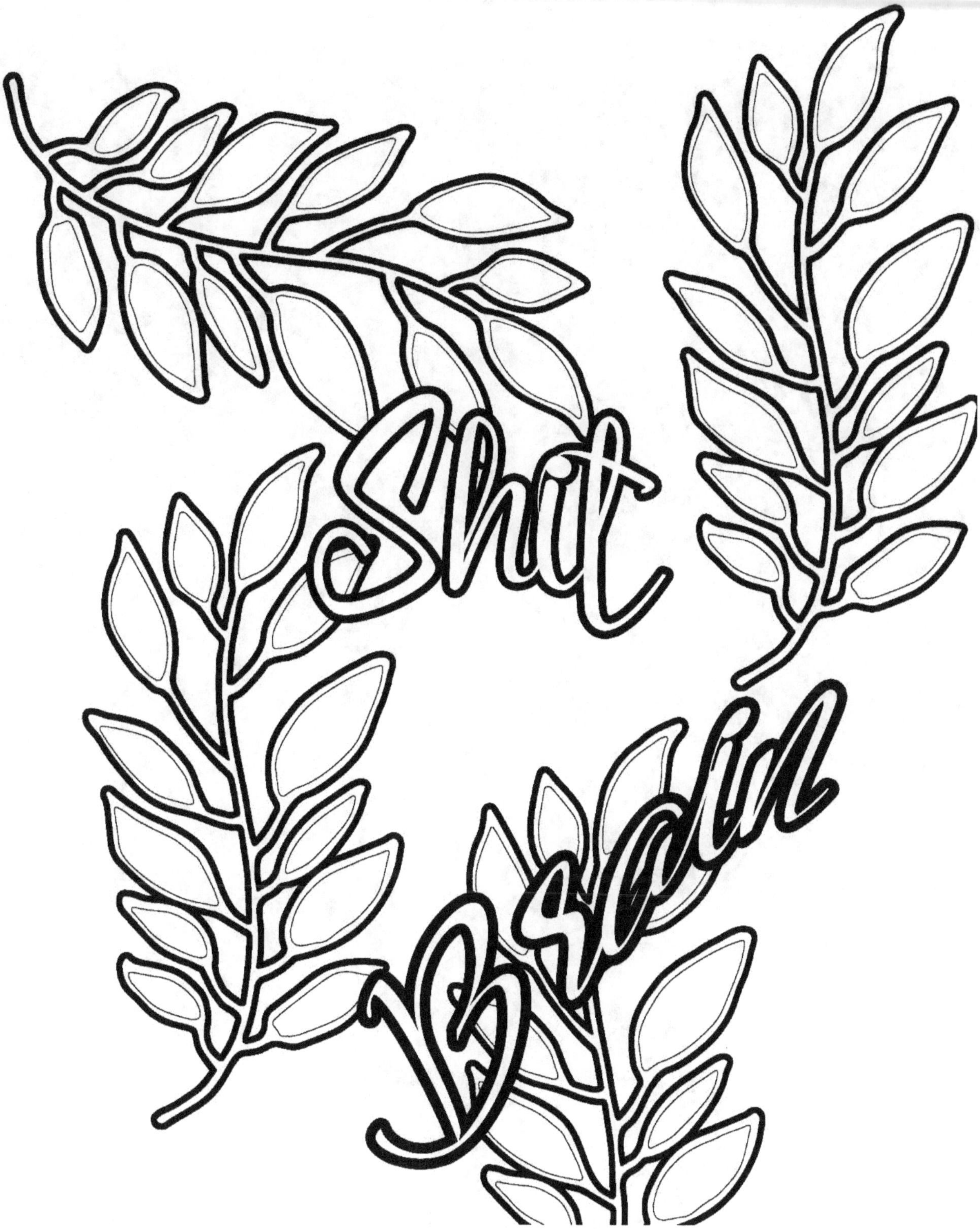
Shit
Brain

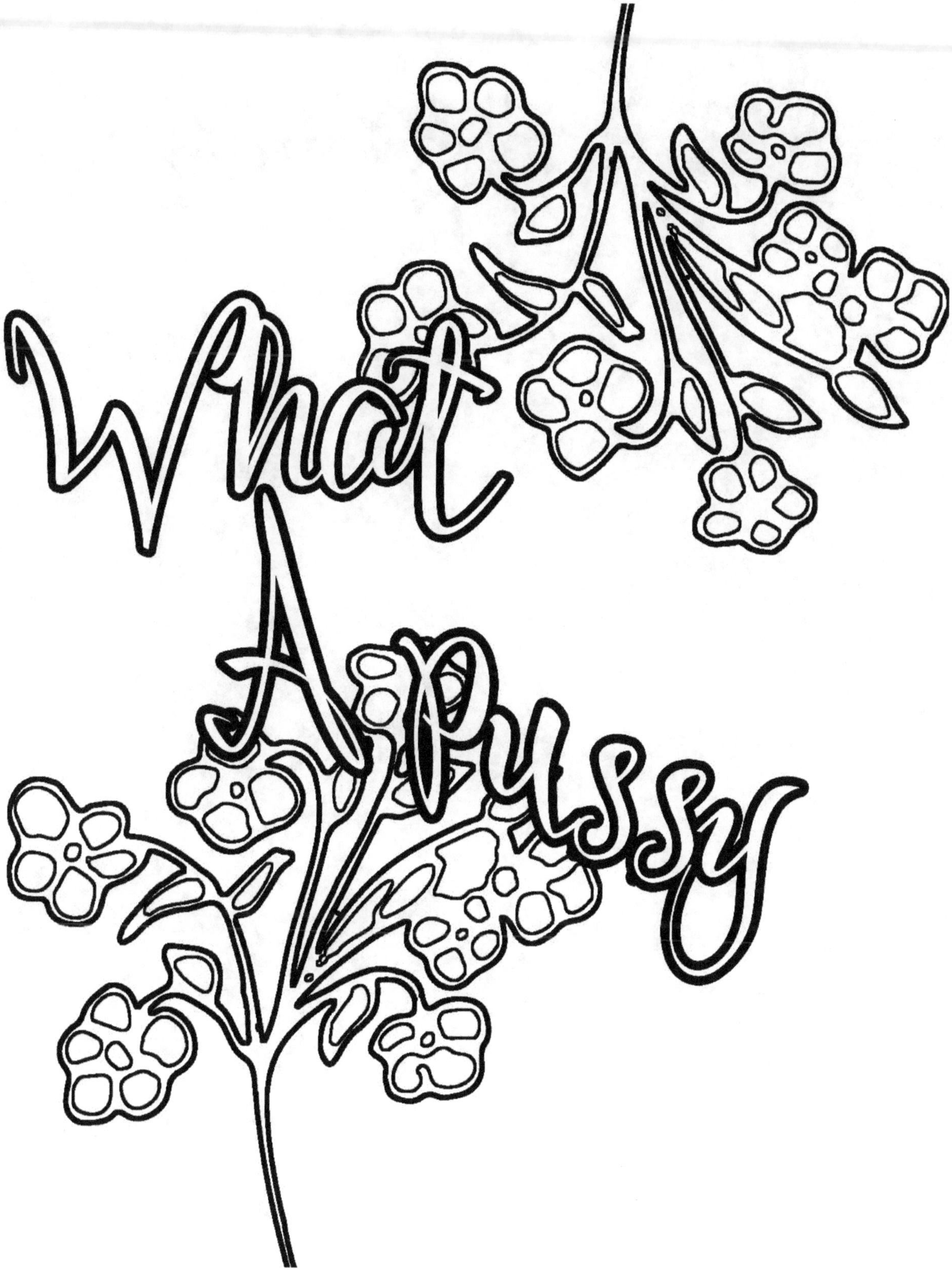
What A Pussy

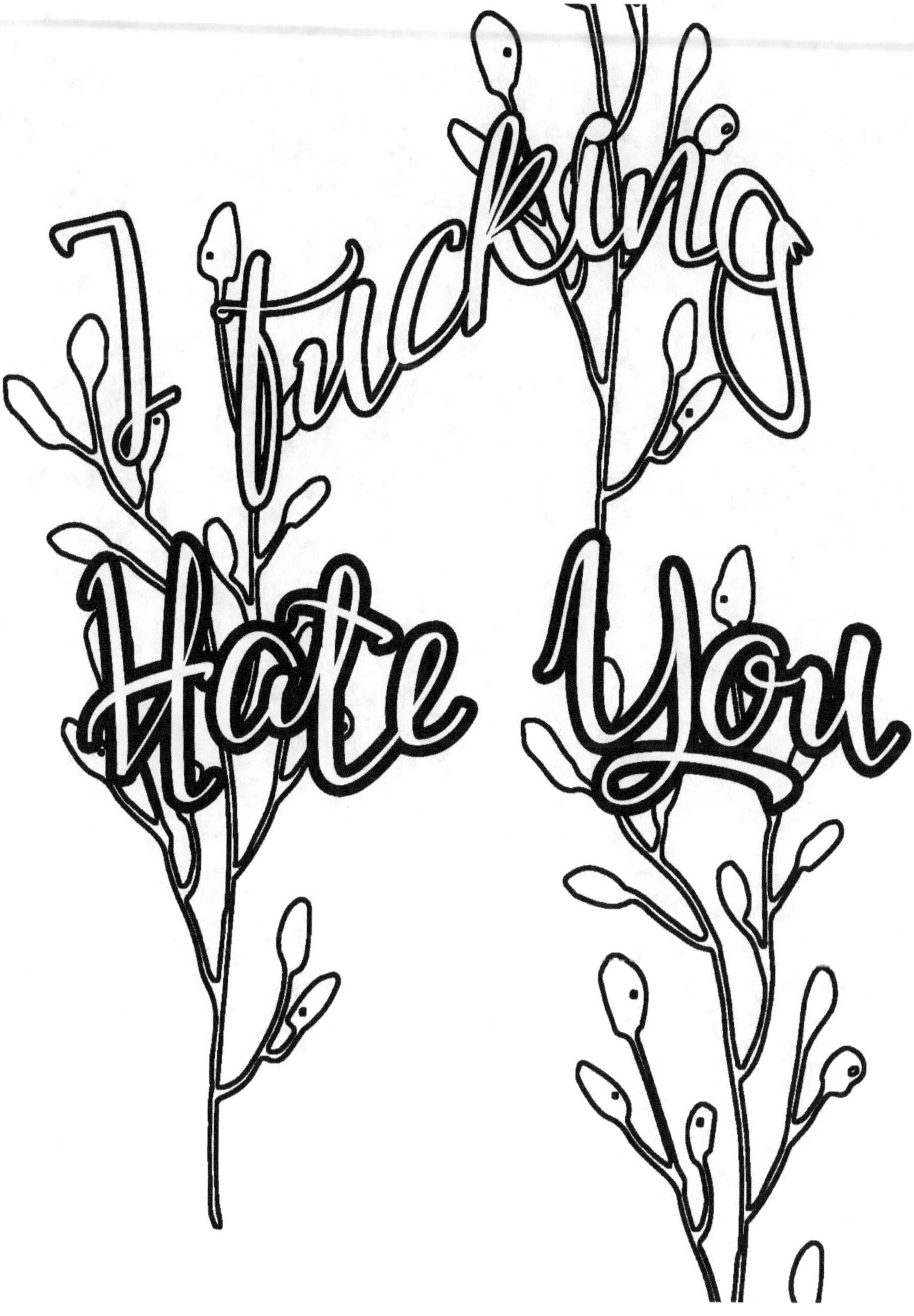
I fucking
Hate You

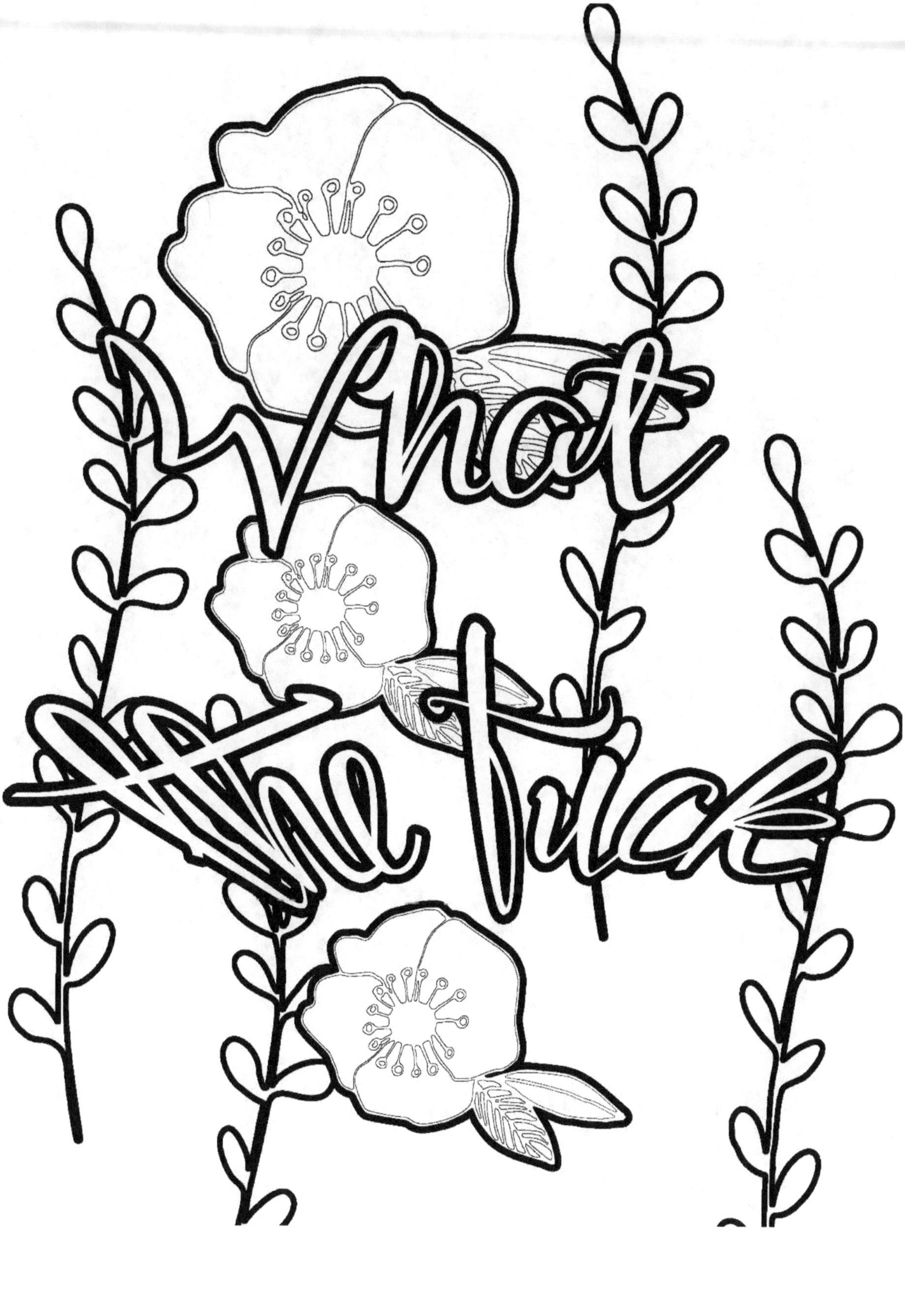
What
the fuck

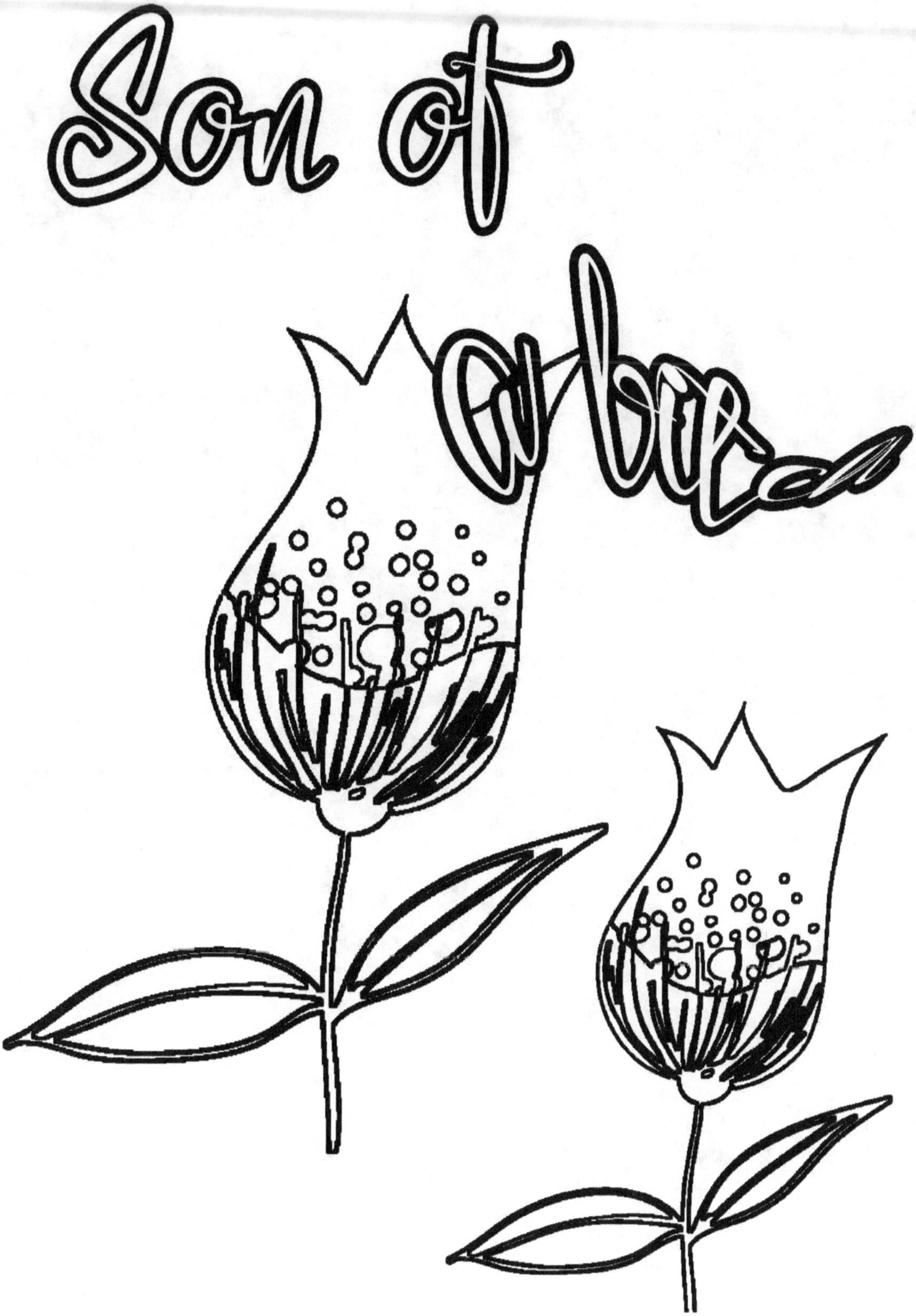
Son of
a bitch

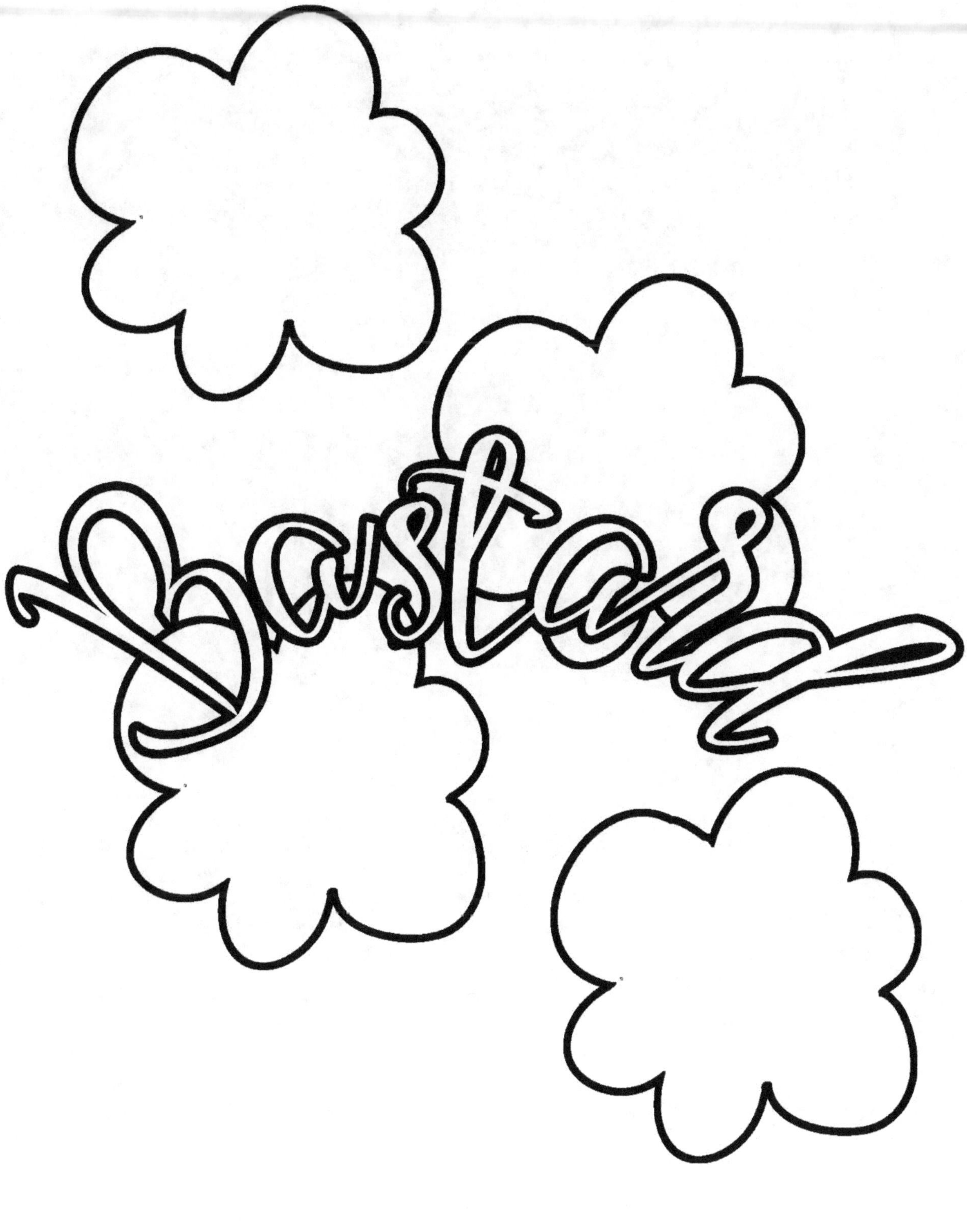
Bastard

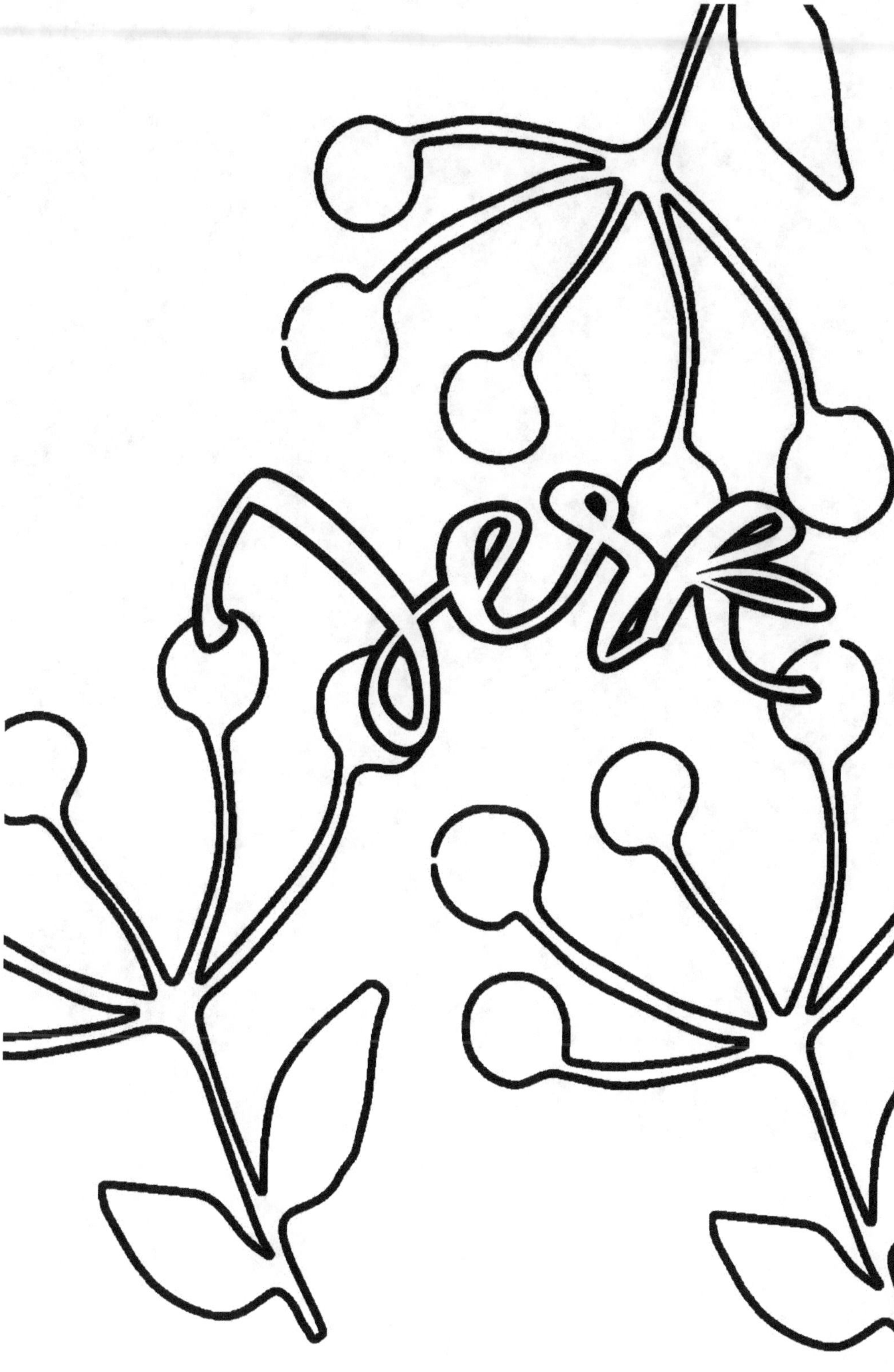
Jerk

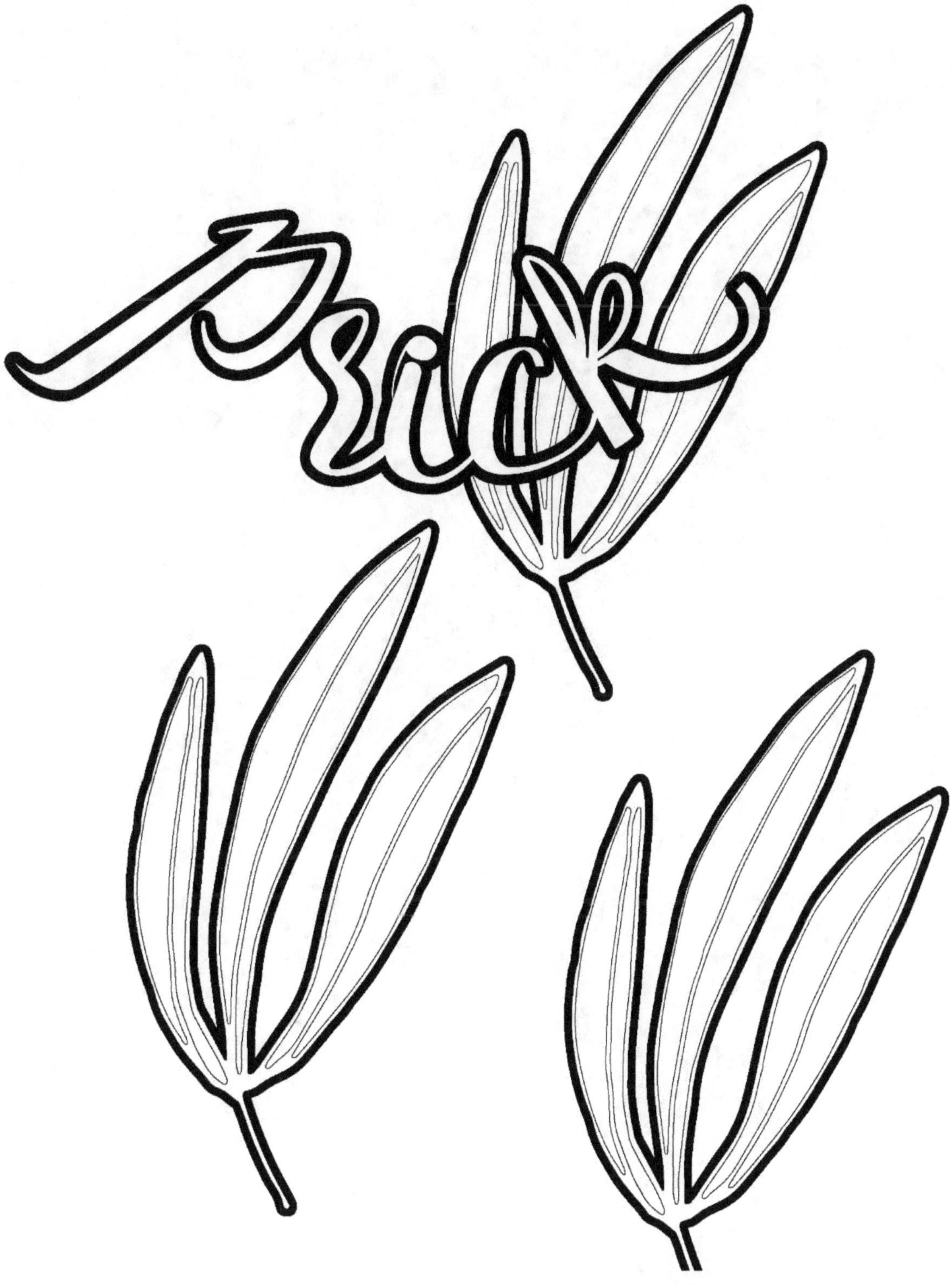
Prick

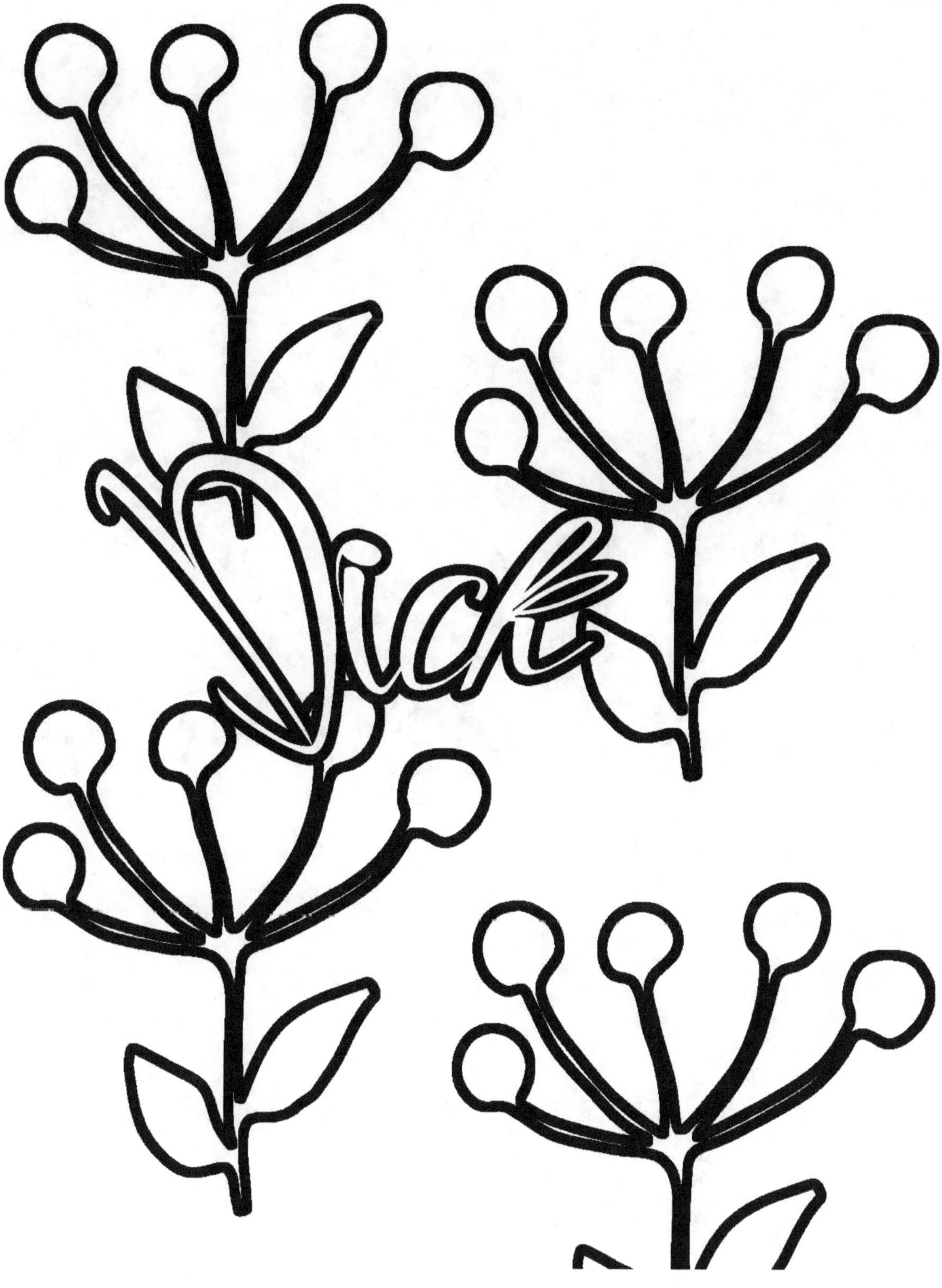
Dick

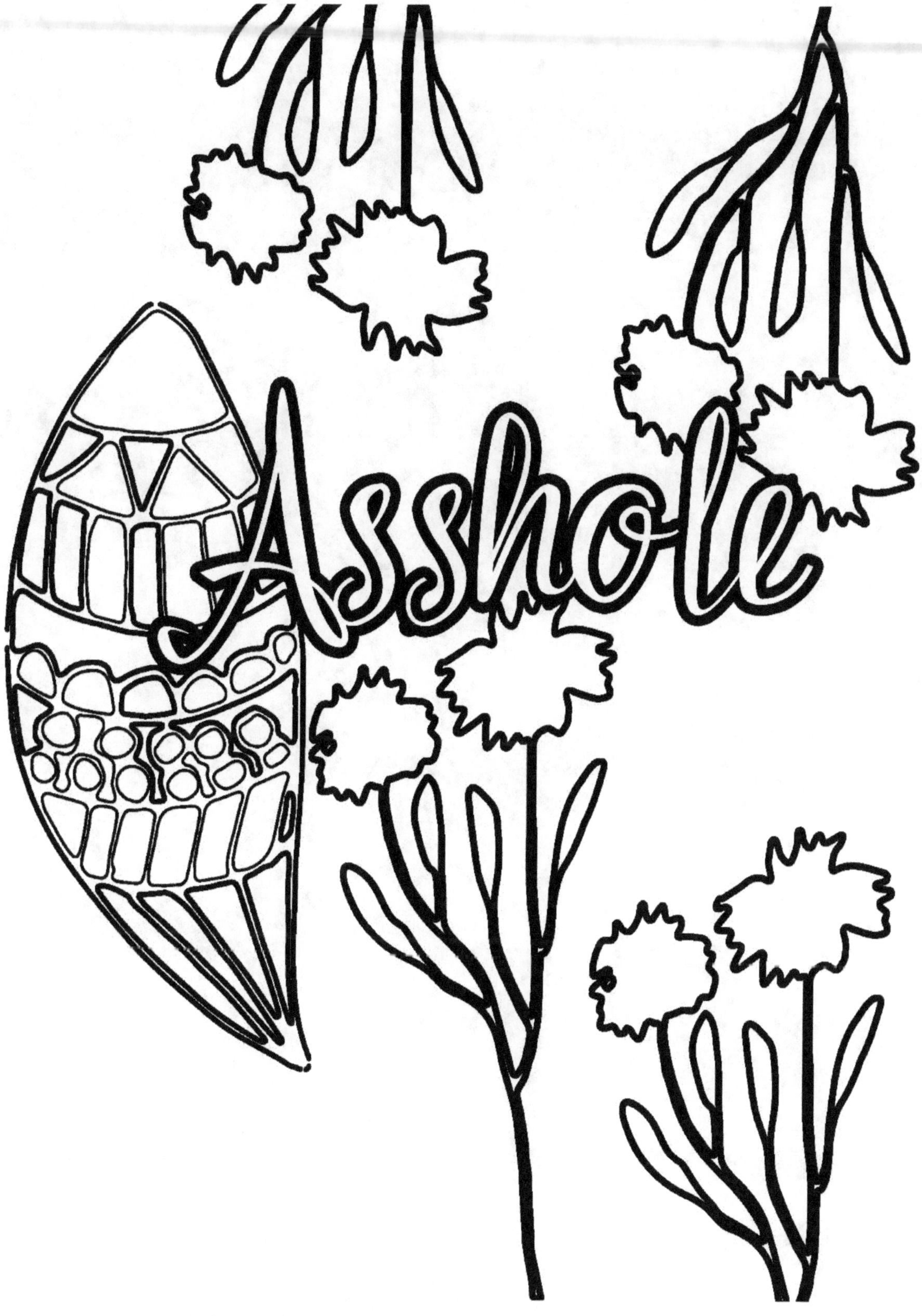
Asshole

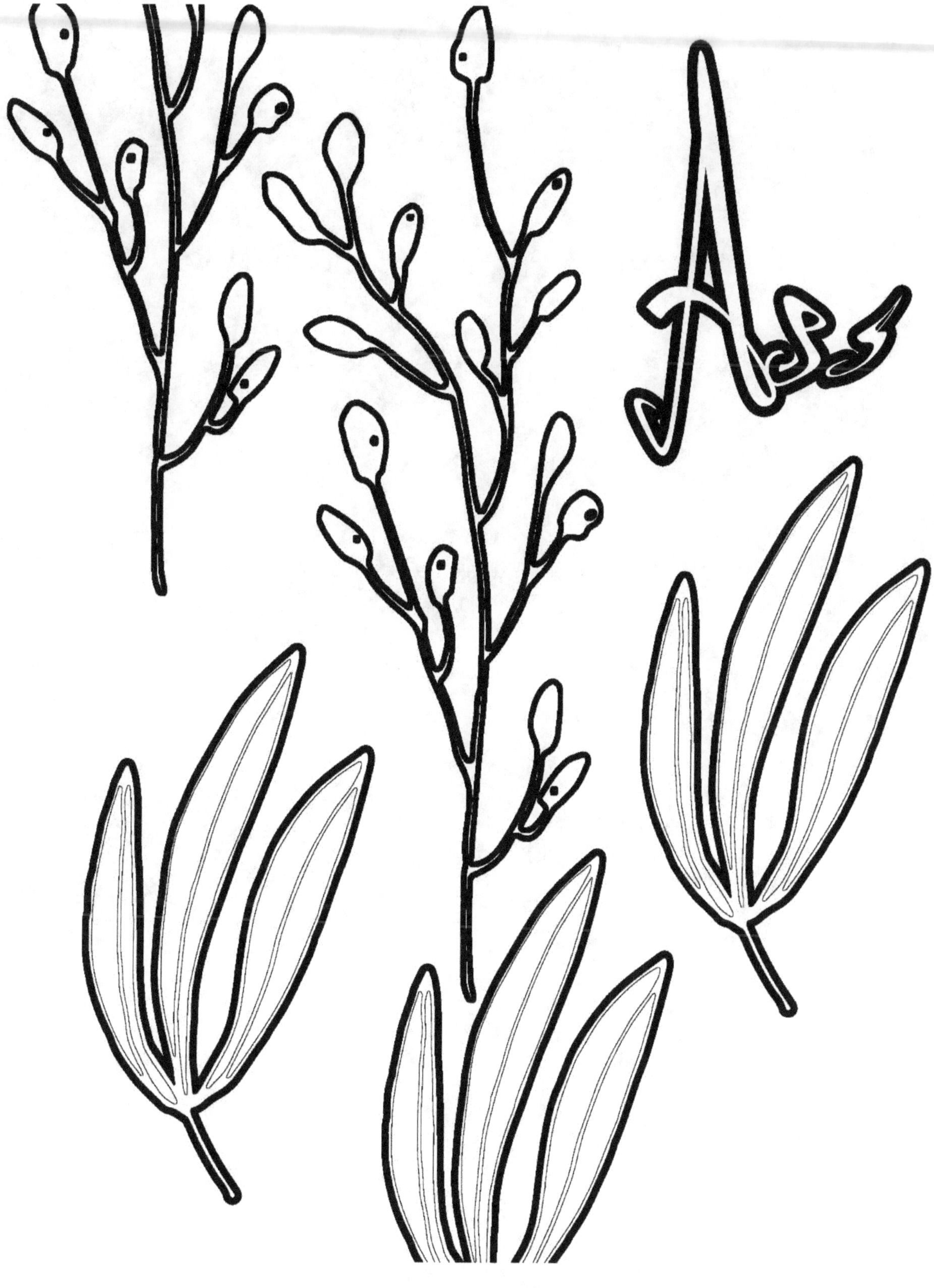
A

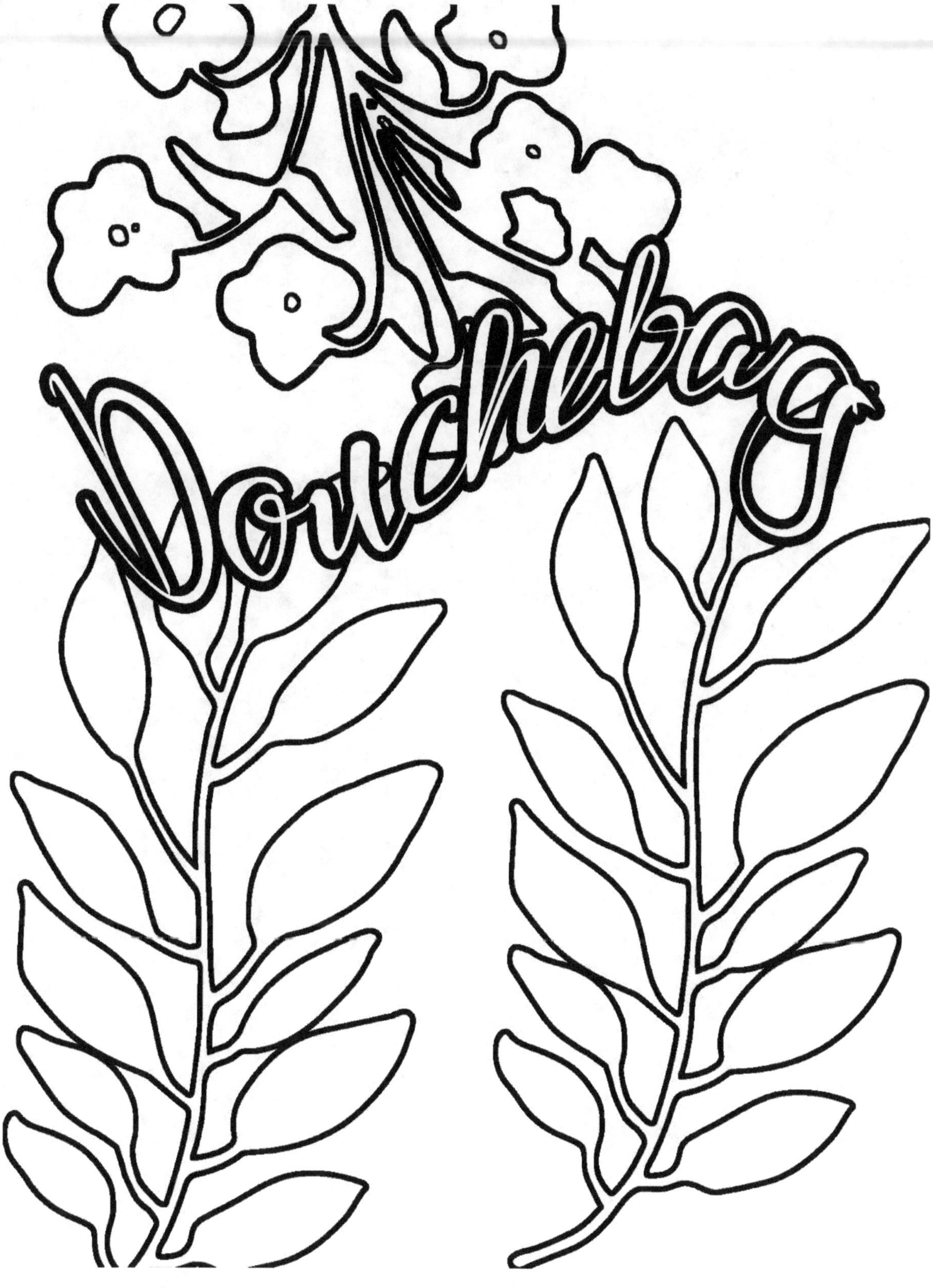
Douchebag

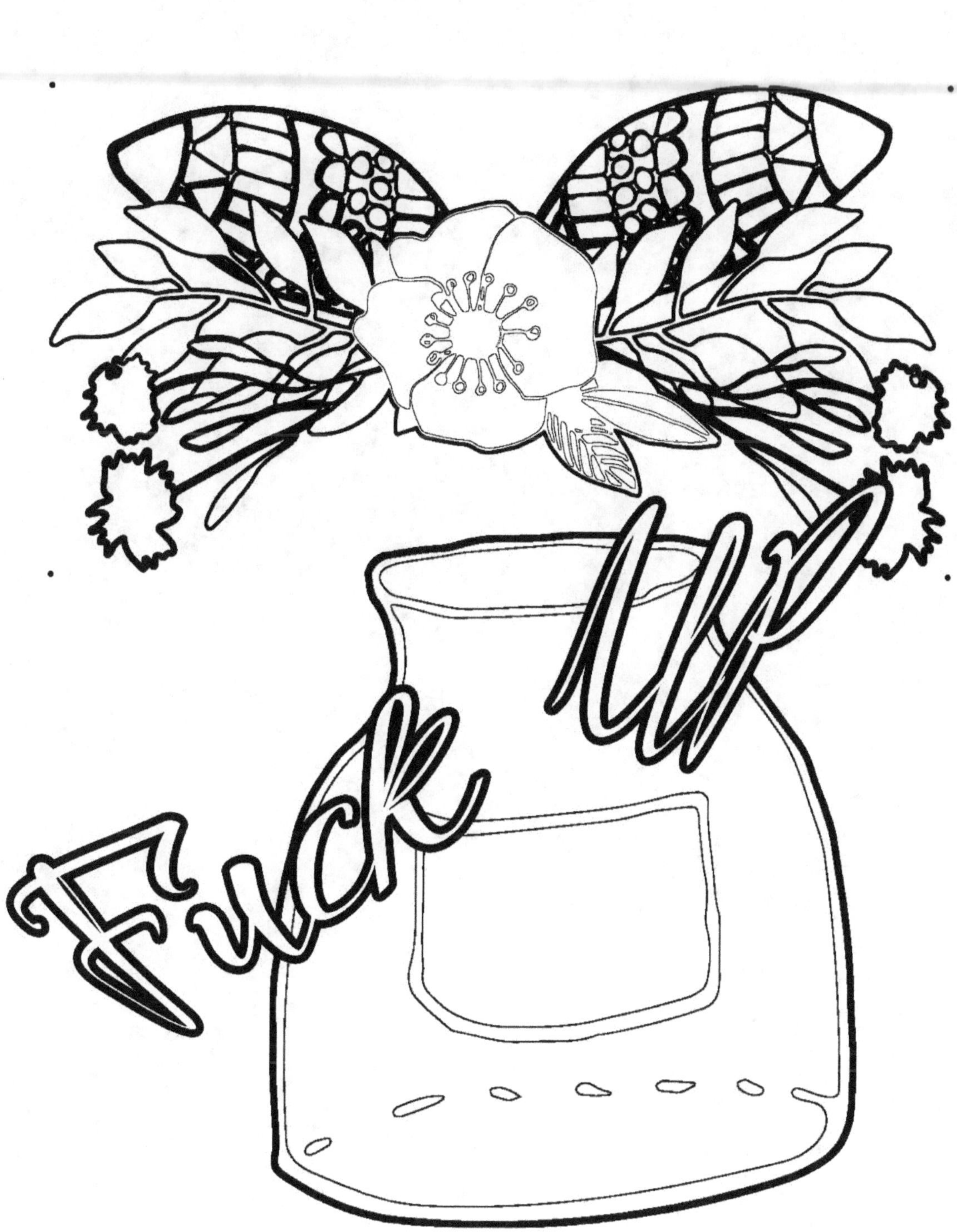

Fuck Up

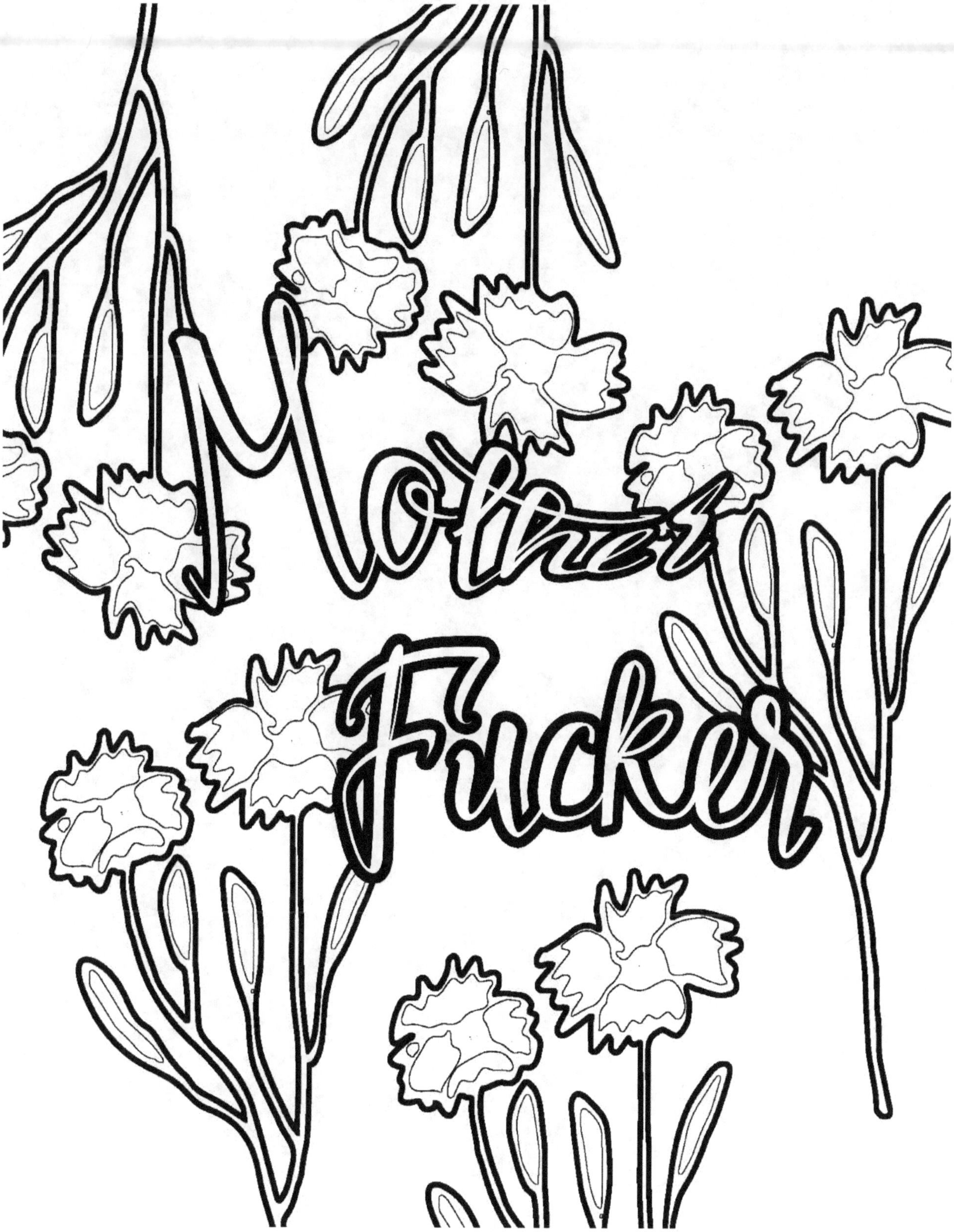
Mother
Fucker

www.ingramcontent.com/pod-product-compliance
Lightning Source LLC
Chambersburg PA
CBHW081123180526
45170CB00008B/2981
9781541179486